Jacqui Rowe

Other Things I Didn't Use To Know

Indigo Dreams Publishing

First Edition: Other Things I Didn't Use To Know
First published in Great Britain in 2020 by:
Indigo Dreams Publishing
24, Forest Houses
Cookworthy Moor
Halwill
Beaworthy
Devon
EX21 5UU

www.indigodreams.co.uk

Jacqui Rowe has asserted her right under the Copyright, Designs and Patents Act 1988 to be identified as the author of this work.
© Jacqui Rowe 2020

ISBN 978-1-912876-35-8

British Library Cataloguing in Publication Data. A CIP record for this book can be obtained from the British Library.

This book is sold subject to the condition that it shall not, by way of trade or otherwise, be lent, re-sold, hired out, or otherwise circulated without the author's and publisher's prior consent in any form of binding or cover other than that in which it is published and without a similar condition including this condition being imposed on the subsequent purchaser.

Designed and typeset in Palatino Linotype by Indigo Dreams.
Cover design by Ronnie Goodyer at Indigo Dreams
Printed and bound in Great Britain by 4edge Ltd.

Papers used by Indigo Dreams are recyclable products made from wood grown in sustainable forests following the guidance of the Forest Stewardship Council.

'All the soarings of my mind begin in my blood.'

~ Rainer Maria Rilke

Acknowledgements

My thanks and love to Raymond Rowe, Claudia Rowe Wright, and Matthew Wright for their unfailing support, both practical and emotional, and for their belief in me; and to Isabel Palmer for her discerning eye on the work, her generosity of spirit, and her friendship. I'm grateful also to Wendy Pratt, whose online courses, when I was returning to poetry and seeking the language to write about my condition, provided a safe and productive space to explore ideas that have found fruition in some of these poems; to Helen Calcutt for great prompts and insights; and to David Calcutt, whose enthusiasm for the poems that I wrote at the earliest stages of this collection has helped keep me going during the more difficult times. Thanks also to my Macmillan counsellor, Pauline, for offering practical solutions when writing seemed insurmountable; to Jonathan Davidson and all at Writing West Midlands for everything they've done for me over the years, and to all in WWM's Room 204 for their fellowship and genuine delight in each other's success; to participants past and present in the Poetry School Birmingham Seminar Group, and in my workshops at the Barber Institute of Fine Arts, many of whom have have been with me from before the start of the journey represented in this book, for their sympathy and understanding. Heartfelt thanks, of course, to Dawn Bauling and Ronni Goodyer for choosing my collection as a winner in the Indigo Dreams competition, for their editing, and for accommodating my particular situation.

If I had not been diagnosed with Chronic Lymphocytic Leukaemia in 2018, these poems would not have existed as they appear here, so I would like to thank my consultant, Professor Paul Moss, and the rest of the staff at the Centre for Clinical Haematology at the Queen Elizabeth Hospital in Birmingham for their kindness, erudition and diligence, and for achieving the amazing feat of helping me derive a positive experience from cancer.

CONTENTS

Spleen 9
I never saw the tree I'd looked at every day 10
Scale 11
small invaders 12
Other things I didn't use to know 13
Wager 14
Declutter 16
You ask me about places 17
Losing 18
What's not worth repairing 19
The creature on my skirt 20
Limulus Polyphemus 21
Diagnosis 22
Does anyone apart from me remember Bucky O'Hare? 23
Obituaries 24
'…on occasions, the gall bladder rather than the heart…' ... 26
River Plasma 27
Universe 28
Epitaxis 29
Elephant's eye 30
Don McCullin 31
Waiting, watching 32

A blood ritual for Samhain	33
Verse before birth	34
Claudia and the trees	35
Travellers' tale	36
Not a Whitsun Wedding	37
Things being various	38
Appointment	39
step	40
Coming off	41
Chemotherapy	42
The sea from Birmingham	44
The source of the Nile	45
Lop-sided	46
No more apoptosis	47
What I might say to my one-time self	48
Not quite the Wars of the Roses	49
Used to	50
What survives	52
Pistyll Rhaeadr	53

Other Things I Didn't Use To Know

Spleen

I fill phials with an homunculus
of blood, watch and wait, mark
each ache as a sign, scour
anatomical maps for the spleen
I didn't know I had until

it was too big to fit the scanner
screen. If I were the sort
of person who liked to name
their parts, I'd call it
Baudelaire. There's too much

white amongst the red. Nodes
are florescent under the shade
of my arms. I've grown this year
an unseen harvest of my own.

I never saw the tree I'd looked at every day

until it turned yellow with autumn, buttery
like the harvest moon, each leaf the colour,
I imagine, of maturing fields. Three storeys high,
the nameless tree, a narrow cone, pointed
towards bonfire night. Had it been a totem, bare
brown in wintery spring? With strings of blossom,
had it been a maypole? When grass was starved
of pigment and I lay here, fevered, curtains drawn
against the heat, what colour was the tree?

Scale

On Brown Clee, I'm bigger
than the sheep, but not by much
when they band together
in the road shade, bigger
than the van below,
than Cleobury, Tenbury
in offline map view.

In slow descent I match cyclists,
dominate hedges, could be people
on the pavements outside
little Sunday-open shops.

Heat dwarfs me. Sheep
are tiny as cat's eyes on the blue hill
and I remember all the tales
when I don't look back, of stopping
for lattice tart we never found again,
of crossing one Clee
or the other in a storm, when
all it was to me was rain.

small invaders

came in the night
uniformly green   while all
the erstwhile growing things expired
in ochre   their bed a patch
of brown too shadowy
for desiccation   threads
of weeds fostered healthy
shoots   as cells divide
and prosper   in bonewalled
gardens   marrowfed   and in closed
darkness propagate   dwell inside   as if
it was their universe this
colossus   me   bestriding
the conquerors' plot

Other things I didn't use to know

Haematology shares a car park
with Maternity; there are eighteen steps to
the front door, I haven't started to use the ramp
yet; *chronic* means slow-growing, *acute* is shorter,
sharper; fever is no more than a number
of degrees; *leuko-* is white, *haemo-* blood itself;
gas and air turns bone marrow
biopsies into fun; Watch and Wait has
quarterly fixtures, always away; blood isn't
one of the Big Four, it skulks in the hinterland
with skin and oesophagus; colours must be
running out, all that's left is orange
for the ribbon and the wristband; you'll
probably die with, not of; survival is measured
in decades, when I hadn't counted on
the plural even while I was well; a book
with *Bloodwise* on the cover, perfect bound,
is mine to keep, a prize, I read it all the way
to Cornwall; Exeter has its own Leukaemia
Fund, but there's nothing in the charity shop
I want; the book talks of equalities, so I can't
be discriminated against now, I laugh; 'cancer'
isn't hard to say at all, as long as it's prefaced by,
'I'm perfectly all right'; people don't always
take in the email or read the whisper; they tell
you how well you look, some suspect you're on
a secret diet; I haven't drawn
a card that gets me out for free.

Wager

Your best bet is to bet on God, said Blaise Pascal –
great name for a *philosophe célèbre* – whether or not
you've been infected by accounts of miracles. Your
extinguishable senses lay on pleasure now but make
no promises of eternal life. Your only hope is living
as if the infinite exists, with all its purgatorial potential.
We believers could have it all wrong, Pascal
would say in his weekly *Pensées* podcast – philosophy,
self-help, the science of happiness – but what else
should we choose if not the currency of faith?
There's no alternative reward. So,

as I go into the centre for the event, I start to think
I didn't lock the car before I've walked here, half
a mile from home. It's not a question. My brain
on steroids can't remember the key in my palm,
my thumb depressing the shut padlock icon, lights
flashing orange, the mirrors gliding in. Even on
50 milligrams, I reason, I never actually left it open.
All the times I've gone back to check, I've found
that my solicitous unconscious has taken on
my repeated obligations, without pestering me
like a puppy, for a pat. Not doing it would be
aberrant, so that's what I'd remember, right? And

anyway, what's in there worth anyone taking,
amongst detritus for recycling – the waterproof
I should have picked up now it's threatening to rain?
My food comes quickly. I can eat it, walk a mile
and still be back in time, just, if I belt along
at performance-enhanced speed. I can't swear
I left the car unlocked, or God exists, but it's still
the only wager in town. From halfway, panting,
up the road, even I see the mirrors turned to clasp
the body, a metaphor for secure. *I locked it,*
I say out loud, trusting my unconscious
to remember this certainty I've outsourced.

Declutter

Other clothes go out, coats I've held onto
until they fitted me again, but they're too big,
too scruffy, just don't look how I look
this time round. I keep the slightly-dated
denim overcoat, heavy, thick, unlined,
could justify the space it takes in terms
of how much less I fill, but instead I say
it's useful for the winter coming, now
there's room for jumpers underneath.

Early in the century I dawdled through Gap
from work to bus, made sure each day this coat
stayed there, in my size but out of my league,
until a cheque came in a letter, the most
I ever earned for just a poem. I scavenge
brooches from discarded collars, pin them
on my prize, a mask, a ship, a metal rose.

You ask me about places

The first thing you ask, of course, is where it is.
I point out the caravan, and how that makes it
Weymouth, then you're riffing on Dorset,
a checklist of places we've been together,
which of them do I remember from
that time before? Haven't you noticed how young
I was? And so was he, on holiday in sports jacket
and tie. My mother must have taken it,
would have been too timid to ask strangers
for a snapshot of the three of us, newly-arrived
in the car he borrowed from his work. *O-O-C! 8-9-3!*
we used to chant – I'd recall more of Dorset
if the places rhymed. And no, I don't know
who those people were, walking down behind,
extras in our dingy period film. What I know
is that I found this picture in a bag of oddments
newer than when my parents were alive. Normally
I'm just like you, into places, histories, but no one's left
to ask, so all I wanted was to keep it in my purse,
me and my dad, my mother a given,
like Dorset, out of shot.

Losing

In the early, unruly, high-dose days, I lose
inches off my hair – to beat the July heat, I swear –
lose reading glasses, then whatever happened between
my purse being in my bag and six feet across
the carpet, lose my left sleeve, lose the chronology
of the past few months, lose any task that I'm
engaged in when the sun glints on something shiny
or a bird trills by the window, lose with pleasure
the restraint that used to stop me talking too loud
and too fast, uttering barbed words to those who push
past me on the shopfront side. When I hear that there's
a footballer called Sokratis, I lose the shame of puns,
*he's philosophical about losing, pass the hemlock,
the unexamined…I'll shut up now,* would like to lose
my aversion to certain well-beloved poets (you don't
have to write it) and villanelles, lose my abhorrence
to the food on my plate, lose the estranged self I don't
want back, lose the thought and thinking it,
the inability to walk up three steps, my body
killing its own red blood, lose the actual strip of pills,
lose the appointment letter, the card I'm supposed
never not to carry, lose whatever
was just in my hand.

What's not worth repairing

One day I might be sitting, light fading outside,
a single lamp to read by, watch or write,
and my beads might trickle down my front,
slipping over tigertail escaped from its crimp,
unclasped from the lobsterclaw, flowing
smoothly, red glass alternately with clear,
as they tumble to the carpet. When I stoop
to pick them up, jumbled in my palm,
the colourless outnumber scarlet. I try
to rethread them, but red white red white
red comes out as white white red white white
white, then white white white white white
white red white, transparent globes
too bulbous to hang straight, balls of ruby
shrivelled to dying berries. Around the room,
transferred roses on the china vase will be
fading into snowy glaze, crimson polka-dots
receding into cushions' unbleached cotton,
white stripes swamping lines of red.

The creature on my skirt

Printed with pink and lighter skies,
he dwells amongst heraldic flowers,
spiky petals, the promise of fruit,
a midnight ground behind prehensile
trees. A leopard in a mosaic coat lies
along a branch, waits to whisk a paw
and shred his shiny monkey skin.
He was woven into this,
aims for where he won't unravel.

Limulus Polyphemus

Still-breathing fossils, horseshoe crabs, not really crabs
at all, have long outlived the asteroid that might have killed
the dinosaurs, the great dyings, the making and breaking
of Pangaea, the End of History. And I'm here too.

Even through my pale-all-year skin it's a stretch to say
my blood is blue. That's where I depart from horseshoe crabs,
so copper-based you cut them and they bleed, not purple,
navy, indigo, royal, but the colour of the optimistic sky.

When the haemocynanin lymph of horseshoe crabs is drawn,
they don't sit in a waiting room for news of platelet levels and
anaemia. Their blue blood, that's kept them fit for 400 million
years or so, has a job to do, the trick of being indispensable.

Once, horseshoe crabs were only good as fertiliser, or
for baiting eels. Now they're gently harvested, scrubbed clean
of barnacles, shells teased back, the elemental powers
of blood drawn with steel needles and exquisite care.

Their amebocytes are primed to sniff out toxins, fix them
in a blue gel cage. What surgically has invaded you,
an organ transplant, drip, the plate that grips my arm,
was swept with blood of horseshoe crabs, made safe.

This immune system I would kill for, but no one seeks to kill
the horseshoe crabs. Once they've yielded a third of their blood,
they're free to go. If their witchcraft could be synthesised,
I read, the 1/12 of them that don't make it home might live.

Home – seawalls crowding out the beaches where they spawn,
overfished as bait, no pampering there or sending back.
Horseshoe crabs survive by being necessary, until someone
replicates their magic, makes it cheaper, more humane.

Diagnosis

I felt better than I'd been for days. *Not leukaemia*
I said, when the appointment came, phoned
to see if it was meant for someone else. I woke
at dawn. Wake up? I hardly slept, or slept for
seven hours, that the next day might come quicker,
not at all. But new doors are always welcome,
surely? *Not leukaemia*, I said. Windows
usually are safer, showing nothing of the world
I'm missing but the sky, or, glancing back,
the face in the glass. *Chronic*, she said, *indolent*.
Something new-conceived and real, tame
until it scratches at my rare, fierce, fought-for
pride, and harder-won contentment. Sometimes
I wish it would leave me to get on with things.
Sometimes I hold it close, my own.

Does anyone apart from me remember Bucky O'Hare?

Not quite an old woman, or so I like to think,
I do have purple hair, and in Costa I tend
to scrape my chair to assail the reveries
of those who wince and groan around me.
When cars on crossings rev and growl at me,
I dawdle, stand beyond the change of lights,
have been known to slap a bonnet, or a few.
With my unrelenting stare, I fix the masses
barging past and never swerve. No one lives
who dares to call me Love or Darling.
(Though, where I come from, Bab
will always be OK) Beware, above all,
my irony. Like Bucky O'Hare, I'm captain
of the Righteous Indignation.

Obituaries

1

But I'm not going to die, I feel obliged to reply,
though I could stumble on the dip in the road as a car
comes round the corner fast. At the traffic lights,
a white van might use the pavement as a short cut
where I'm waiting, and I'd stand my ground.

Where I is Incurable and T is Terminal in the expression
$I \neq T$, I type the joke about prognositicated years
being better than I would have dared hope before
I was ill. Ill. Honestly, I say, it's no more than
a never-ending cold and I'm not going to die of that,
with hat, gloves for the bus, and Vitamin C.

But one day one of us will notice that another
hasn't posted for a while, won't ask, yet,
then someone we hardly know will be disseminating
details of the celebration of that life, whose account
will stay, the profile photograph unageing like a poet
famous in the 1980s, and sometimes people we haven't
met will comment on it how much they still miss us,
will dash off a poem but not post one of ours.

2

Someone has died who had the same as I have,
had it ten years, someone once famous, a useful
point of reference when no one recognises the initials,
so now I can say, *CLL, the same as he had, you remember?* But
what everyone remembers best is his long acceptance triggered
by diagnosis, preparation for the end, the chronic span
of dialogue with death, the refusal to give in that toyed
with the inevitable, how waking of a morning can be
unexpected, and sometimes, yes, I know, that seems hard
won. I can cite a 69.3% chance of surviving a decade,
but what they want to hear is the poem he wrote
about staying alive long enough to see the tree.

'...on occasions, the gall bladder rather than the heart...'
(Oxford Professor of Poetry Public Lecture, Simon Armitage)

It wouldn't be stylised on a birthday card,
pinned to a teddy bear's chest. I picture it
as the leather pouch I keep my random
words in, a mermaid's purse of stones
too low on the Moh's index to be of value,
as a bilirubin shade on an edgy decorator's
colour card, as the plastic bag I flushed
my aqueous insides into when the duct
was stoppered and I turned dirty ochre.

This organ is no use to anyone, the surgeon says,
a fossil, wasting breath and blood. His mission
to straighten out the sloppiness of evolution,
he makes it sound like mending, snip a hole,
haul it out, stitch it up, conscious alteration
permanent as a tattoo, a covert badge of agency.

It's less destined to be grave goods
than my Mercian hoard of quartz
and silver rings, or the steel riveted to the ulna
my receding skin will leave behind, being
that I am of shed and arrival, my atoms
palpitating in space for so much longer
than the memory of pain.

River Plasma

Plasma is like a river, says the article.
I hope it is my midland river, flows through
Shrewsbury, Bridgnorth on a market day, doesn't
burst its banks round Tewksbury. I hope
it meets the Stour from Clent,
the Vyrnwy from Powys, the Avon
and the Arrow, and the lovely Wye
that wanders through Rhyadar
and Builth Wells, then home
to Hereford and on. I hope the platelets,
waterfowl, will bob along my Severn's course
as it gushes to the Bristol Channel
and the sea.

Universe

There's gold in blood – the wine of heroes
who battled gods, Egyptians said – but much more
meagre than a scrape from your wedding ring,
not enough to start a rush on graveyards.
You contain 25 trillion red blood cells,
give or take, each 25,000 times smaller
than a grain of sand. And there are maybe
only 100 billion stars across the 100,000
light years of the Milky Way, if you wanted
to claim that you contain a universe.

Each red cell treks 300 human miles,
on a journey to its bucket list of vena cava,
atria, ventricles, bicuspids, aorta,
kidneys, trunk and limbs, a four month
road trip, stumbling towards the climax,
the fabled sepulchres of the liver
and the spleen.

Epitaxis

        Toilet paper, pristine,
      limp, the shame of explanation
       gushing from my bag,
    nothing like on
        cult TV where
       alien encounters, time
displacement, telekinesis,
           telepathy, the potential
    for death,
      incite cosmetic
haemoglobin
      painted on
   like lip gloss, viscous,
       straight
    from the nostril, neat,
       stopping
           just short of the mouth,
     other worlds away from
       these unruly
   scarlet splashes
          with nowhere to hide
on the puzzle of my frock,
          raspberry jelly
     coagulating
  in my throat,
      dried stigma
        on my palm.

Elephant's eye

Sometimes I think I remember the wobble
of my pram, the view of pavements kneeling up,
but what I'm certain of is consciousness
was christened up the hill to my grandmother's,
in pink stripes on new socks my mother
warned me not to dirty, as I ran up and down
the steps to where the gardens sloped away
and houses behind them were higher still.

Then there's a break. I can't bring back
what we had for dinner, or being on the bus,
but as the usherette I've furnished out of
photographs of foyers, in a dark red Odeon
greatcoat, shone a shaded torch on lightless
rows of swinging seats, a rope like the outline
of a balloon was spinning against a sky
in colour on the wall-sized screen.

I kept watch for it to appear again, that swirling loop,
and when it did, *this is where we came in,* my mother
jumped to put her coat on and mine, needing
to get home to do my father's tea. On the bus back
I used the words I'd picked up, *surrey, territory,* sang
of cowmen, farmers, mavericks, perhaps, except that
I'm not sure of anything but the hoops on my socks
and that lasso, higher than all the houses on the hill.

Don McCullin

In my teens, I never noticed
that the pictures were in black and white.
For a month or so, I wanted to be
a war photographer, I, who didn't go abroad
until I was twenty-two, and then to France.
I wanted to be you, though,
and when I see you on BBC4,
relentlessly immersed in greys, the image
emerging in grainy red bulb light, and only
then you know you've got it right,
patience I never had in the days
of waiting days to go to Boots
to pick up the wallet of inevitable
disappointment, I still want to be you,
even though I have a phone
where I can lay on afterwards a choice
of monochromes, impose the shape,
the ratio of faces, I want to be you
in your eighties, climbing to whatever height
it takes to make the angle, you leaping
up to faith that what you see will fade
to paper from your thought, exact.

Waiting, watching

I'm watching the progress of foliage
on tall trees that might be sycamores,
their branches exposed crown first,
like old prints of the nervous system, waiting
for the bus that never comes, then
there are three, sluggish as my blood in these
darkening days. I'm watching shadows
petrify the spongy cloud, waiting for the sun
to barricade itself behind them, watching
tongues of rusty leaves, fuchsia
droplets, purple and magenta, waiting
by the roadworks traffic lights for red
to let me cross, watching orange daub
the high street, waiting in the half-term
queue behind plastic pumpkins, picturing
phlebotomists got up as vampires.

A blood ritual for Samhain

Ghostbusters is playing on the radio
and she can't find a vein in either arm.
I want to watch the blood come out
today, I say, it being Halloween.
My elbow crooked and braced, I don't flinch
at the needle, thin as hair, embroidering me
with spiders' webs. A dribble in the tube
is hopeful. Not enough, she says. *It might only
be a smear,* I think, *but it's life and death…*

She's telling me she never looked away
when they took bloods from her mother
and that's what made her want to do this job.
She gives up arms, will have to try my hand,
and I'm behind the sofa, blotting out the thought
of juicy veins that stand proud like
a vampire's road map. My other hand
across my eyes, the point still feels
driven home. Avoiding the wound,

I watch two phials fill up. She hopes
that will do and as she sticks on cotton wool
I want to say *It's practically an empty arm,*
but she's too young, or has had it
said to her too many times.

Verse before birth

One I would not see. I grasped her close inside
and turned away, said *Good day*, but didn't look
until there were two. Clinging to my hard-found
joy, I waited there for three, for her, though
they were always pair by pair, and I might
have loved a boy as much. Silver sometimes
fluttered near, but never gold. I asked
for no secrets I'd hold too tight,
wishes and kisses still far away.

Claudia and the trees

A woman keeps phoning the BBC, I said.
We laughed, and put the baby to bed at the front,
in the room watched over by the oak, whose height
and girth the people before had parlayed
into eighteenth century. She slept as fitfully
as the clatter of leaves, I dreamt through gusts,
and branches looming between the streetlight
and the curtains.

Next day I pushed the tiny pram
that held her month-long length, for the daily exercise
of keeping me from Neighbours and the news.
So much was changed since September just gone
that twigs on the tarmac, bins upturned, odd bricks,
were not as odd as my altered state, or hers,
of being planted here and growing sturdy.

She kept that room until, some nights, she said,
The trees are falling on me, and though the oak
only groaned, we moved her to the back.

Travellers' tale

There'd be no communication, even though
they all had mobile phones by then. I got
a new and edgy notebook, to write down
what she missed – the title of the coming
Harry Potter, the next Pirates – left Dirty Dancing
where she had left it, rending the video recorder
useless for that silent month. I had prayed
she'd come away from the presentation
saying, *Not for me*, but hadn't I colluded
in what made her fearless, hungry for places?

When we watched Blue Peter after school,
film of cold children ploughing upwards in the dark,
the presenter still shaken, Kilimanjaro the hardest
thing he'd ever done, it was too late for me to beg,
her name was down, deposits paid. *You'll only hear
from us*, the organiser said, while I was taking
photographs of her logo t-shirt, and the kit I'd been
too scared to go with her to buy, *if it's all gone wrong.*

Each day, the joy of hearing nothing. Until
one night past eleven, the dog was barking
at the window, someone on the path. I should have
gone and got it over with, the breaking of the silence,
but I left it to her father, while I listened for the tones,
sinking to the lowest stair. Then the door shutting.

Pizza delivery, he said. *Come to the wrong house.*
To say that this mistake has never ever happened
before or since, doesn't make it any less
an anticlimax, but her traveller's tales, of sun rising
on the mountain and the trip to Zanzibar,
could never thrill me quite as much
as the other story: *Come to the wrong house.*

- 36 -

Not a Whitsun Wedding
For Claudia Rowe Wright and Matthew Wright

In some years, though, this weekend would
be Pentecost. On the lawn, a shower, not
of arrows, real flowers shot from cannon,
and the rain, thank goodness, chose yesterday
to block the lanes, or we'd all be covering
our fascinators, and sighing how we nearly
died by sinking into mulch. Girls in green
satin, and the bride's man, wait to group
for photographs, once *les Français* are done,
les cousins, les tantes, les beaux-frères. Later,
a couple of us will sing along to *Oh, Champs-Elysées*
in lieu of bilingual conversation, drinking cider,
this last summer of us all being part of the main. Then
the string quartet plays *Game of Thrones*,
another final season, marked in barns like this,
and village halls and manor houses across all of Hereford
today, and way beyond, celebrations as unknown
to each other as tomorrow's WhatsApp photographs
of two new rings, and, at tables named for your beloved
creatures out of fantasy, this evening's speeches
declaring that to quench the universe's thirst,
the pair of you just had to be.

Things being various
'Snow' Louis MacNeice

All my life I've hated snow, the way it snarls
the city, promising the winter will be long
enough to annexe spring. Sometimes,
in the flame of summer, MacNiece seduces me
with his crazier world, flakes multiplying more
than anyone could know, out there behind
the glass, beyond the roses, where we'll
quarter tangerines by the bubbling fire. But really
I'm the woman stranded on the pavement, with
a poundshop umbrella that buckles at the hint
of blizzard, by the claggy road, no certainty
of getting home now the buses have stopped,
no one prepared, none of this forecast,
world just as sudden as we think.

Appointment

When I get out at the clinic, the taxi driver
says he'll pray for me. He's asked me, for his knowledge,
what they do here, where he's dropped
so many off before, and I've used my cheerful self
as the example, *I'm OK, honestly,* talking too fast
in case he has the nerve to call me brave.

I've dressed to look as if I've come in
for a meeting, gratified when the receptionist
doesn't need my letter to know my name,
old hand that I am in Phlebotomy, practised
in identifying my best vein, saying, *take
whatever extra blood you need for research.*

Then the wait for processing I've come prepared
for with my iPad and a book, patient while
others grouch. Called in, I ask questions like a swot,
the star pupil who doesn't cry when the levels
this time aren't so good. *Must try harder,*
I go out thinking, take the bus home.

step

slow step
one step after
blood clock
dragging one beat
slower beat
thought drags
to earth
slow earth
only earth earth
mother me
in slow darkness
moon gone stars
gone slower
than trees

Coming off

A while ago, the Year of Famous Deaths
and those not quite so celebrated, around the time
when Carrie Fisher went, I saw an alien craft
approaching in the dark, until I realised,
white and liquid, it was only Venus.

But harbingers are vague and retconned.
Fatigue, no appetite, nausea, diarrhoea, mood
swings, what are these not symptoms of?
Betelgeuse is growing dim, I'm told,
and could become a supernova shortly.

And I'm living on my body fat again. Diviners
probe my sucked-out marrow. My time approaches
to explode, but someone tells me always how good
I look. Maybe I'm a semi-variable, no longer
in the Top 10 brightest seen from here.

Chemotherapy
Alfred Gillman, Louis Goodman & Gustav Lindskog

Seeking antidotes, that this new war should not
be drowned in gas, they dig into the records,
30/09/18, phosgene, chlorine, fallout from
the fifth Ypres, probably, west of Passchendaele
and hell, the Battle of the Peaks, ten thousand
wounded, ill, and here a gunner with no white
blood cells. If gas can kill the healthy, what might
it do for the bad? They digress from weapons, see it
work on animals, find a volunteer, JD, all that's left
of him, jaw wired by a tumour, arms pinned
by swollen nodes, locked in a cancer shell, inject him,
August '42, with Substance X, synthetic, lymphocidal.
Mustard gas. He eats, sleeps, revels in the respite
when the pain abates, dies in the December.

Never saw
Stylised seahorse, Staffordshire Hoard

he that fashioned me
        never saw the deepest sea
    knew great horses dwelt in foam
  ships long-headed gallopers
          screwed wire into filigree
waves that rolled in the old songs
    he that never saw the depths of sea
      took filaments
    airy hairs of gold from ultra mare
twisted them finer than my eye
      a cry for wind a sword a prayer
    he that spilled me never saw the sea
      but trusted in a horse's snout a sword the soil
      they never saw the sea who fought
        for me but dreamed of stallions with
tails of fish like twisted rope
        told round the golden fire old tales
of filigree like waves and spry
        and then they
    buried me

The sea from Birmingham
Tate St Ives

The road's awash today,
buses cut through shallows,
spray beats on the side of vans,
water pools in pot holes.
On the corner, in a handful
of rain, a hint of brine, and I see
split screen, other light, warm
sand, land rising, brushy green,
in dusky glass. Myself in maps
of mirror cubes, reassembled
with a cloud, a sail. In a window
frame, planes of cobalt, Prussian,
flake white blending into ochre,
grey, the flag an accent
on the golden mean,
ultramarine.

The source of the Nile

In Denbigh, Henry Morton Stanley offers his hand,
the topi from the Wikipedia photographs in the other.
Perhaps locals know to grasp his fingers for the luck
he found away from here, perhaps they mutter
I presume as they walk past, praying for others
who wander, lost. Back at the car, I tell you about
the clumsy effigy, and the promised rain is starting
as we set out in search of another lake, Anwyn…Aylwen…
somewhere…but all of the signs point to Bala. *Denbigh
is a breed of sheep,* I say, and *I remember I was with you
in Ruthin once.* If either is true, I have no way of knowing.
Probably, he never said it. Meeting the sick man on
the shore of Tanganyika, even Lake Victoria a dead end,
will have knocked all the glib rehearsal out of him.
.

Lop-sided

How long before *autoimmune* or *cancer* entered
my vernacular was my body out to get me?
If mutation's the foundation of evolving,
there are going to be slips, too much division
and not enough death. Take one, or several,
for the species: my right leg longer than
the other, one shoulder higher, one breast
heavier, hair sparser on the left, lop-sidedness
a leitmotif in adolescent photographs, hidden
painstakingly at my wedding. And then the colds,
so continuous they might have been only one,
from my first breath as far as my last gasp,
augmented by a choking cough my grandmother
said was from the graveyard.

No more apoptosis

Beyond the festivals that burn
a path for winter, when trees should
decently be turning skeletal to pose
against the bleached-out sky
on non-committal Christmas cards,
leaves still adhere to branches, drooping
eyelids, ochre, russet, bred just now
to throw themselves at storms.

Oaks and sycamores, beech,
ash, chestnuts, lime, in thrall
to chlorophyll no longer, turn out
gold, turn out more of it
and more, an unfallen coup-d'état
declaring, the first time since
Persephone was trapped in hell,
there will no more be seasons.

What I might say to my one-time self

I don't know the future, any more than
you do, but I'm sure it doesn't turn
on a single act; eradicating one specific
sacrifice or solitary protest would not
wipe out a movement. So I'm not
going to suggest you change your diet
or your mind, choose some other subject,
live in a different town, refuse the offer,
run a mile. Where I am now is where
you still would be, here in this place
that all the histories have formed for us.

Not quite the Wars of the Roses

Was it Tewksbury, where three suns shone
on the son of York, and put an end to one
of many Edwards? Or was it Wakefield, where
a Richard of York got battered in vain? Or
Mortimer's Cross, where yet another Edward,
Earl of March, began his march to kingship?
Might it have been death-soaked Towton? Or
a further Richard on his way from Bosworth
to the carpark, horses fled, crown
on a bramble bush, a Henry at last?

Which battle, exactly, am I waging? So-called
forces ranged against me being liveried in white,
I could throw in my colour with Lancastrians, as if
I cared to be the she-wolf, two-handed on my useless
broadsword, leading the bloody charge against something
smaller than a speck of dust, whose only mission,
to survive, is nothing less than mine. And I would
raise an army to stamp out what I can't see,
can't call an enemy?

I have decades down this line, I'm told,
in static altercation. If, when my obituary appears,
it depicts a final battle, which I lost,
remember I was always *hors de combat,*
never in it for the fight.

Used to
Inspired by conversations in Herefordshire care homes

Have I told you this before, what we used
to do? On Saturdays, we'd go to Kington
for the dances. Like Paris it was then.
Miles and miles, there and back, I'd walk
those days. Summer, we'd give them a hand
picking the hops. It was a different world

in those days, our own little world.
Our neighbour had a motorbike. He used
to take us wimberrying, Jessie and me. Hands
were black as night when we got back. Kington,
that's where everybody went, a good walk
but I saved my money, we didn't have much then.

Three o'clock, tea'll be round soon. Then
there was hop-picking, best fun in the world,
when they threw us girls into the crib. I'd walk
for miles in those days, did I already say? I used
to remember all of it once. Mr Slater from Kington,
have I told you about him? He only had one hand

and he drove the taxi. Safe as anything, his other hand
was. Jessie and me we were best of friends, then
she went to Rotherwas to make the bombs. Kington
never was the same without her, another world,
and she was yellow when she came back, used
some funny stuff there, they did. I'd walk

for miles, I still do, most mornings, walk
to Hereford, and in these slippers, too. Hand
me my cup, I'm a bit shaky today. Mam used
to shout at us for going wimberrying, then
I'd have to black the grate. Never saw the world,
never went to Rotherwas, but we had Kington.

I met my Bernard at a dance one Saturday in Kington.
Sometimes of a Sunday he'd take me for a walk
down by the Wye after church. He was the world
to me. Courting we were, we'd go hand in hand.
After he went, the house and all was all sold up, then
they sent me here. It's all right when you get used

to it, a little world of our own and they say Kington
isn't far. I used to dance there. I'd like to go for a walk
and hold somebody's hand, same as it was then.

What survives

Side by side they lie in dusky soil, Alice and Carlos,
the lady and her swain. Hard to know which
is which, both chipolata bodies over-stuffed,
one dark, one fair, their bristly hair rubbed
clean on saddles of cracking skin, both snouts
dwarf planets in their perfect roundness, all eyes
not quite existent, ears providing shade,
tails not curly-whirly, chunky as a dog's.
With their train of flies, they grind and grunt
up to the fence, jolting each the other, expectant
of thrown fruit and vegetables the painted
sign allows. None comes. They shrug, resume
their stately lying, a monument to all that remains:
grouchy, enforced, companionable fidelity.

Pistyll Rhaeadr

One of our birthdays in a cold July, looking for food
up creeping lanes across the border,
we found a waterfall.

Or rather read the signs and didn't quite believe
the road would open out, there'd be a carpark
and a stream, a café.

Opposite, the skein suspended, whiter than the sky,
its motion more substantial here
than wall or bough or leaf.

Water generated smells of diesel,
drizzle, foliage damp with summer
to the point of rot.

Inside they'd lit a fire, too warm to sit too close,
and I took off my parka for the first time
since we left.

They offered bara brith and welsh cakes, the malted
heat of dark tea, amongst voices bemoaning
the loss of another year.

And I wondered how it would be to not go back tonight,
to lie and listen to pale water dropping,
so that we would never fall.

Indigo Dreams Publishing Ltd
24, Forest Houses
Cookworthy Moor
Halwill
Beaworthy
Devon
EX21 5UU
www.indigodreams.co.uk